INSTRUMENTAL PLAY-ALONG

CD+ INSIDE

G000129144

Top Hits from
TV, Movies & Musicals
INSTRUMENTAL SOLOS

Arranged by Bill Galliford and Ethan Neuburg
Recordings Produced by Dan Warner, Doug Emery and Lee Levin

© 2016 Alfred Music
All Rights Reserved. Printed in USA.

ISBN-10: 1-4706-3301-9
ISBN-13: 978-1-4706-3301-1

Alfred

Contents

MP3 CD Track

Song Title	Page	Demo	Play-Along
Tuning Note (A Concert)			1
All About That Bass	4	2	3
Glee / Meghan Trainor			
As Time Goes By	7	4	5
Casablanca			
Arthur's Theme (Best That You Can Do)	8	6	7
Arthur / Christopher Cross			
Blueberry Hill	10	8	9
The Man Who Fell to Earth / Fats Domino			
Both Sides Now	11	10	11
Love Actually / Joni Mitchell			
Boulevard of Broken Dreams	12	12	13
American Idiot / Green Day			
Can You Feel the Love Tonight	14	14	15
The Lion King / Elton John			
Concerning Hobbits	15	16	17
The Lord of the Rings: The Fellowship of the Ring / Howard Shore			
Can't Fight the Moonlight	16	18	19
Coyote Ugly / LeAnn Rimes			
Cool Kids	18	20	21
Glee / Echosmith			
Corpse Bride (Main Title)	19	22	23
Corpse Bride / Danny Elfman			
Diamonds Are Forever	20	24	25
Diamonds Are Forever / Shirley Bassey			
Falling Slowly	21	26	27
Once / The Swell Season			
Ding-Dong! The Witch Is Dead	22	28	29
The Wizard of Oz			
Don't Stop Believin'	24	30	31
The Sopranos / Journey			
Fame	26	32	33
Fame / Irene Cara			
Follow the Yellow Brick Road/We're Off to See the Wizard	27	34	35
The Wizard of Oz			
For Your Eyes Only	28	36	37
For Your Eyes Only / Sheena Easton			
Goldfinger	29	38	39
Goldfinger / Shirley Bassey			
Ghostbusters	30	40	41
Ghostbusters / Ray Parker, Jr.			
Gonna Fly Now (Theme from *Rocky*)	32	42	43
Rocky / Bill Conti			
The Good, the Bad and the Ugly (Main Title)	34	44	45
The Good, the Bad and the Ugly / Ennio Morricone			
The Great Escape March	36	46	47
The Great Escape			
The Greatest Love of All	37	48	49
The Greatest / Whitney Houston			

ALL ABOUT THAT BASS

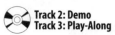

Track 2: Demo
Track 3: Play-Along

Words and Music by
MEGHAN TRAINOR and KEVIN KADISH

All About That Bass - 3 - 1

INSTRUMENTAL PLAY-ALONG

CD+ INSIDE

Top Hits from
TV, Movies & Musicals
INSTRUMENTAL SOLOS

Arranged by Bill Galliford and Ethan Neuburg
Recordings Produced by Dan Warner, Doug Emery and Lee Levin

© 2016 Alfred Music
All Rights Reserved. Printed in USA.

ISBN-10: 1-4706-3301-9
ISBN-13: 978-1-4706-3301-1

Alfred

Alfred Cares. Contents printed on environmentally responsible paper.

Contents

ALL ABOUT THAT BASS

Track 2: Demo
Track 3: Play-Along

Words and Music by
MEGHAN TRAINOR and KEVIN KADISH

Moderately bright (♩ = 132)

All About That Bass - 3 - 1

AS TIME GOES BY

(from *Casablanca*)

Words and Music by
HERMAN HUPFELD

ARTHUR'S THEME
(BEST THAT YOU CAN DO)
(from *Arthur*)

Words and Music by
BURT BACHARACH, CAROLE BAYER SAGER,
CHRISTOPHER CROSS and PETER ALLEN

Moderately slow, with a half-time feel (♩ = 68)

Arthur's Theme (Best That You Can Do) - 2 - 1

Arthur's Theme (Best That You Can Do) - 2 - 2

BLUEBERRY HILL

Words and Music by
AL LEWIS, VINCENT ROSE
and LARRY STOCK

Moderately slow (♩. = 92)

BOTH SIDES, NOW

Words and Music by
JONI MITCHELL

BOULEVARD OF BROKEN DREAMS

Words by
BILLIE JOE

Music by
GREEN DAY

Boulevard of Broken Dreams - 2 - 1

Boulevard of Broken Dreams - 2 - 2

CAN YOU FEEL THE LOVE TONIGHT

(From Walt Disney's *The Lion King*)

Track 14: Demo
Track 15: Play-Along

Words by
TIM RICE

Music by
ELTON JOHN

CONCERNING HOBBITS

(from *The Lord of the Rings: The Fellowship of the Ring*)

Music by
HOWARD SHORE

Track 16: Demo
Track 17: Play-Along

CAN'T FIGHT THE MOONLIGHT

(from *Coyote Ugly*)

Words and Music by
DIANE WARREN

Can't Fight the Moonlight - 2 - 1

COOL KIDS

Track 20: Demo
Track 21: Play-Along

Words and Music by
GRAHAM SIEROTA, JAMIE SIEROTA,
NOAH SIEROTA, SYDNEY SIEROTA,
JEFFERY SIEROTA and JESIAH DZWONEK

Moderate rock (♩ = 126)

Track 22: Demo
Track 23: Play-Along

CORPSE BRIDE
(Main Title)

Music by
DANNY ELFMAN

Track 24: Demo
Track 25: Play-Along

DIAMONDS ARE FOREVER

Music by JOHN BARRY
Lyric by DON BLACK

FALLING SLOWLY

(from *Once*)

Words and Music by
GLEN HANSARD and
MARKÉTA IRGLOVÁ

Track 26: Demo
Track 27: Play-Along

DING-DONG! THE WITCH IS DEAD

(from *The Wizard of Oz*)

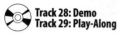

Track 28: Demo
Track 29: Play-Along

Music by HAROLD ARLEN
Lyric by E.Y. HARBURG

Ding-Dong! The Witch Is Dead - 2 - 1

Ding-Dong! The Witch Is Dead - 2 - 2

DON'T STOP BELIEVIN'

Words and Music by
JONATHAN CAIN, NEAL SCHON
and STEVE PERRY

Don't Stop Believin' - 2 - 1

Don't Stop Believin' - 2 - 2

Track 32: Demo
Track 33: Play-Along

FAME
(from *Fame*)

Lyrics by
DEAN PITCHFORD

Music by
MICHAEL GORE

FOLLOW THE YELLOW BRICK ROAD/
WE'RE OFF TO SEE THE WIZARD

(from *The Wizard of Oz*)

Track 34: Demo
Track 35: Play-Along

Music by HAROLD ARLEN
Lyric by E.Y. HARBURG

Track 36: Demo
Track 37: Play-Along

FOR YOUR EYES ONLY

Music by BILL CONTI
Lyrics by MICHAEL LEESON

Track 38: Demo
Track 39: Play-Along

GOLDFINGER

Music by JOHN BARRY
Lyrics by LESLIE BRICUSSE
and ANTHONY NEWLEY

Moderately ($\quarternote$ = 104)

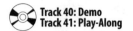

GHOSTBUSTERS

Words and Music by
RAY PARKER, JR.

Who you gon-na call? Ghost - bust-ers!

Who you gon-na call? Ghost -

bust-ers!

Ghostbusters - 2 - 1

Ghostbusters - 2 - 2

31

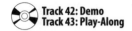
Track 42: Demo
Track 43: Play-Along

GONNA FLY NOW
(Theme from *Rocky*)

Words and Music by
BILL CONTI, AYN ROBBINS
and CAROL CONNORS

Moderately ♩ = 96

Gonna Fly Now - 2 - 1

THE GOOD, THE BAD AND THE UGLY
(Main Title)

By ENNIO MORRICONE

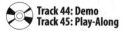

The Good, the Bad and the Ugly - 2 - 1

The Good, the Bad and the Ugly - 2 - 2

Track 46: Demo
Track 47: Play-Along

THE GREAT ESCAPE MARCH

(from *The Great Escape*)

Words by
AL STILLMAN

Music by
ELMER BERNSTEIN

Moderate march (♩ = 116)

THE GREATEST LOVE OF ALL

Track 48: Demo
Track 49: Play-Along

Words by
LINDA CREED

Music by
MICHAEL MASSER

HE'S A PIRATE

(from Walt Disney Pictures' *Pirates of the Caribbean: The Curse of the Black Pearl*)

By KLAUS BADELT

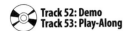

HEDWIG'S THEME

(from *Harry Potter and the Sorcerer's Stone*)

Music by
JOHN WILLIAMS

*A♯ = B♭

I DON'T WANT TO MISS A THING

(from *Armageddon*)

Track 54: Demo
Track 55: Play-Along

Words and Music by
DIANE WARREN

I Don't Want to Miss a Thing - 2 - 1

I Don't Want to Miss a Thing - 2 - 2

IN DREAMS
(from *The Lord of the Rings: The Fellowship of the Ring*)

Words and Music by
FRAN WALSH and
HOWARD SHORE

JAMES BOND THEME
(from *Dr. No*)

By
MONTY NORMAN

Track 58: Demo
Track 59: Play-Along

Track 60: Demo
Track 61: Play-Along

From Walt Disney's Frozen
LET IT GO

Music and Lyrics by
KRISTEN ANDERSON-LOPEZ
and ROBERT LOPEZ

Let It Go - 3 - 1

THE MAGNIFICENT SEVEN
(Main Title)

By ELMER BERNSTEIN

Track 64: Demo
Track 65: Play-Along

NOBODY DOES IT BETTER
(from *The Spy Who Loved Me*)

Music by MARVIN HAMLISCH
Lyrics by CAROLE BAYER SAGER

THE NOTEBOOK
(Main Title)

Written by
AARON ZIGMAN

Slowly, with expression (♩ = 69)

Track 68: Demo
Track 69: Play-Along

OVER THE RAINBOW
(from *The Wizard of Oz*)

Lyric by
E.Y. HARBURG

Music by
HAROLD ARLEN

ROAR

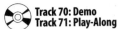
Track 70: Demo
Track 71: Play-Along

Words and Music by
KATY PERRY, LUKASZ GOTTWALD,
MAX MARTIN, BONNIE McKEE
and HENRY WALTER

Moderate pop rock (♩ = 90)

Verse 1:

Verses 2 & 3:

Chorus:

Track 72: Demo
Track 73: Play-Along

THE PRAYER

Words and Music by
CAROLE BAYER SAGER and DAVID FOSTER

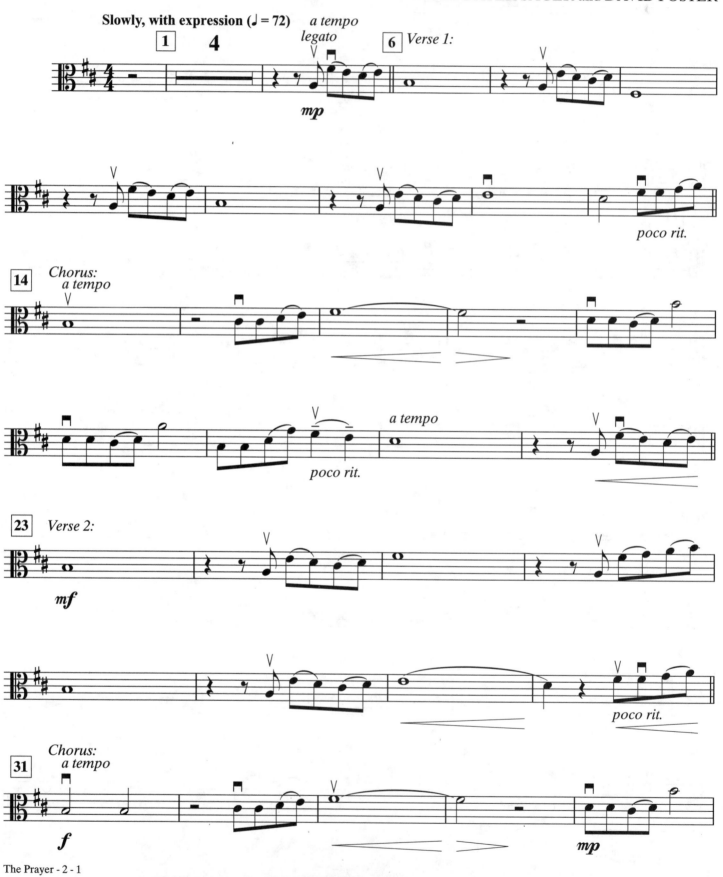

The Prayer - 2 - 1

The Prayer - 2 - 2

(I CAN'T GET NO) SATISFACTION

Track 74: Demo
Track 75: Play-Along

Words and Music by
MICK JAGGER and KEITH RICHARDS

SONG FROM M*A*S*H
(Suicide Is Painless)

Words and Music by
MIKE ALTMAN and JOHNNY MANDEL

Track 78: Demo
Track 79: Play-Along

SEE YOU AGAIN

(from *Furious 7*)

Words and Music by
CAMERON THOMAZ, CHARLIE PUTH,
ANDREW CEDAR and JUSTIN FRANKS

See You Again - 2 - 1

STAIRWAY TO HEAVEN

Words and Music by
JIMMY PAGE and ROBERT PLANT

Stairway to Heaven - 2 - 1

STAR WARS
(Main Theme)
(from *Star Wars Episode IV: A New Hope*)

Track 82: Demo
Track 83: Play-Along

Music by
JOHN WILLIAMS

Majestically, steady march (♩ = 108)

SUMMERTIME

(from *Porgy and Bess*)

Music and Lyrics by
GEORGE GERSHWIN,
DuBOSE and DOROTHY HEYWARD
and IRA GERSHWIN

Track 84: Demo
Track 85: Play-Along

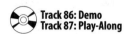

THEME FROM SUPERMAN

Music by
JOHN WILLIAMS

Theme from Superman - 2 - 1

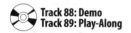
Track 88: Demo
Track 89: Play-Along

WE ARE YOUNG

Words and Music by
NATE RUESS, ANDREW DOST,
JACK ANTONOFF and JEFFREY BHASKER

We Are Young - 3 - 1

66

We Are Young - 3 - 3

YOU ONLY LIVE TWICE

Track 90: Demo
Track 91: Play-Along

Music by JOHN BARRY
Lyric by LESLIE BRICUSSE

Moderately slow (♩ = 84)

Track 92: Demo
Track 93: Play-Along

A WHITER SHADE OF PALE

Words and Music by
KEITH REID and GARY BROOKER

Moderately slow ♩ = 76

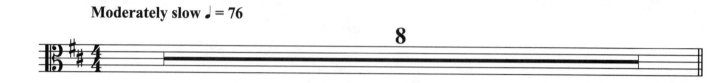

A Whiter Shade of Pale - 2 - 1

A Whiter Shade of Pale - 2 - 2

THE WINDMILLS OF YOUR MIND

(from *The Thomas Crown Affair*)

Track 94: Demo
Track 95: Play-Along

Words by
ALAN and MARILYN BERGMAN

Music by
MICHEL LEGRAND

The Windmills of Your Mind - 2 - 1

The Windmills of Your Mind - 2 - 2

Track 96: Demo
Track 97: Play-Along

YOU RAISE ME UP

Words and Music by
ROLF LOVLAND and
BRENDAN GRAHAM

YOU'VE GOT A FRIEND IN ME
(from *Toy Story*)

Words and Music by
RANDY NEWMAN

INSTRUMENTAL SOLOS

This instrumental series contains themes from Blizzard Entertainment's popular massively multiplayer online role-playing game and includes 4 pages of art from the World of Warcraft universe. The compatible arrangements are carefully edited for the Level 2–3 player, and include an accompaniment CD which features a demo track and play-along track. Titles: Lion's Pride • The Shaping of the World • Pig and Whistle • Slaughtered Lamb • Invincible • A Call to Arms • Gates of the Black Temple • Salty Sailor • Wrath of the Lich King • Garden of Life.

(00-36626) | Flute Book & CD | $12.99

(00-36629) | Clarinet Book & CD | $12.99

(00-36632) | Alto Sax Book & CD | $12.99

(00-36635) | Tenor Sax Book & CD | $12.99

(00-36638) | Trumpet Book & CD | $12.99

(00-36641) | Horn in F Book & CD | $12.99

(00-36644) | Trombone Book & CD | $12.99

(00-36647) | Piano Acc. Book & CD | $14.99

(00-36650) | Violin Book & CD | $16.99

(00-36653) | Viola Book & CD | $16.99

(00-36656) | Cello Book & CD | $16.99

LICENSED BLIZZARD ENTERTAINMENT PRODUCT

Harry Potter

INSTRUMENTAL SOLOS

Play-along with the best-known themes from the Harry Potter film series! The compatible arrangements are carefully edited for the Level 2–3 player, and include an accompaniment CD which features a demo track and play-along track.

Titles: Double Trouble • Family Portrait • Farewell to Dobby • Fawkes the Phoenix • Fireworks • Harry in Winter • Harry's Wondrous World • Hedwig's Theme • Hogwarts' Hymn • Hogwarts' March • Leaving Hogwarts • Lily's Theme • Obliviate • Statues • A Window to the Past • Wizard Wheezes.

(00-39211) | Flute Book & CD | $12.99

(00-39214) | Clarinet Book & CD | $12.99

(00-39217) | Alto Sax Book & CD | $12.99

(00-39220) | Tenor Sax Book & CD | $12.99

(00-39223) | Trumpet Book & CD | $12.99

(00-39226) | Horn in F Book & CD | $12.99

(00-39229) | Trombone Book & CD | $12.99

(00-39232) | Piano Acc. Book & CD | $18.99

(00-39235) | Violin Book & CD | $18.99

(00-39238) | Viola Book & CD | $18.99

(00-39241) | Cello Book & CD | $18.99